Everyday Costume
in Britain

Everyday Costume in Britain

From the Earliest Times to 1900

Audrey Barfoot

B. T. Batsford Ltd. London

© Audrey Barfoot 1961
First published 1961
Fourth impression 1968
Fifth impression 1972

ISBN 0 7134 1901 6

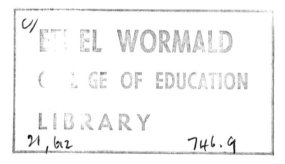
Printed and Bound in Great Britain
by C. Tinling & Co. Ltd, London and Prescot
for the Publishers
B. T. BATSFORD LTD
4 Fitzhardinge Street, Portman Square, London, W.1

Contents

Introduction

Generalizations are invariably dangerous. Nevertheless, after a detailed study of costume, certain conclusions seem inescapable.

A pictorial graph of the development of fashion might go straight ahead from the primitive wearing of skins to the introduction of textiles but, once styles had been evolved, the line of the graph would describe a series of circles, implying that, suitably adapted, there is virtually nothing completely new in fashion except the introduction of modern synthetic fabrics, which provide fresh and exciting possibilities. Even so, the basic cut of garments may usually be related to a fashion popular many years before. For example, practical hooded cloaks have existed since Roman–British times; but now, translated into plastic, they are basically the same. Medieval capes and sleeves crop up in Victorian times; sack-backed dresses were mentioned by Samuel Pepys; the attractive comfort of a full-skirted dress has been recognized in all periods, and the modern shirt-waister dress has triumphantly survived successive invasions of sack dresses and narrow tubular skirts.

A knowledge of costume gives the student a comfortable feeling of 'know how' on seeing an accurately produced historical play or film. Conversely, he or she will cast a knowledgeable, critical, and perhaps disapproving eye over theatrical productions showing inaccurate period costume. A useful hint for those designing costumes for pageants or plays is that while characters in Court circles, particularly the young dandies, should be dressed in high fashion current at a specified date, the older, more conservative, characters and poorer countryfolk may safely be dressed in costumes about ten years behind the times. Apart from a general reluctance to adopt new-fangled ideas, communications were slow and there was no literature such as fashion magazines. Except for a brief period about 1770, children wore miniature copies of adult clothes; consequently, few are illustrated here.

History can be made a dull catalogue of dates and battles; but it is really the story of people, and costume is an essential part of their everyday life.

Note: The numbers in parentheses in the text refer to the page numbers of the illustrations.

1 Pre-Roman Britain

Archaeological remains provide no evidence of spinning and weaving earlier than the Bronze Age (1900 to 750 B.C.). Because of the perishable nature of textiles, it is uncertain precisely when the Northern tribes began to wear cloth instead of animal skins cleaned and softened with flint scrapers, and sewn with bone needles threaded with animal sinews.

Traces of flax and woollen fabrics have been found in Early and Middle Bronze Age graves, with jewellery including Yorkshire jet belt-rings, bronze ornaments, blue Egyptian beads, Baltic amber, and Irish gold. A chieftain of about 1300 B.C. was buried in a magnificent sheet-gold shoulder-cape, resembling the PELERINE shown on Page 17. Men and women wore necklets, armlets, and collars or TORQUES of amber, bronze, gold, or shale. Social classes included priests, traders, miners, smiths, artisans, warriors, and peasants, who probably wore caps, tunics, and cloaks like those found in Denmark.

Page 9 shows a Neolithic or Stone Age man wearing a primitive garment of skin. The Romans called tribes beyond the pale of Roman civilization 'Northern Barbarians'. The Bronze Age man wears belted and cross-gartered leather breeches or BRACCATAE; these distinguished barbarians from Romans, whose legionaries subsequently wore them knee-length beneath their tunics. They resembled Tudor CANIONS(39). A small square of leather or coarse wool, folded diagonally, covers the man's shoulders; he had learned to make rough skin moccasin-type shoes. The Bronze Age woman wears a belted woollen tunic, which could be either long or short, over a woollen KIRTLE; this is the origin of the modern custom of wearing a slip beneath a dress. A square blanket is fastened on her shoulder with a clasp or buckle.

By 54 B.C. crafts had developed, speeded by more highly civilized settlers from what is now Europe. Britons were proficient at weaving and dyeing coarse woollen cloth, rough on one side, in stripes and checks, probably the origin of tartans and plaids. The Ancient Briton wears woven under- and over-tunics, trousers, leather shoes, and a cap of fur or wool. The warrior wears a short tunic under a sleeveless fur jumper, with cross-gartered breeches.

Women, proud of their long hair, wore it flowing or in plaits. The British woman wears a belted tunic and a cloak fastened with a FIBULA or brooch. Archaeological evidence shows that Early Bronze Age men and women used low, conical jet buttons in the Mediterranean fashion. During the Late Bronze Age they followed the northern Europeans' preference for large ornamental pins.

Materials	Skins, linen, coarse woollens.	**Furs**	British native wild animals.
Colours	Dull blue, red, and black.		

STONE AGE MAN "NORTHERN BARBARIANS"

ANCIENT BRITONS 54 B.C.

9

2 Roman Britain 54 B.C.–A.D 410

The Roman conquest of Britain entailed many expeditions over many years, due to the islanders' stubborn resistance and guerrilla tactics reinforced by Belgae and Gauls. Crafts had developed particularly in south-east Britain during the Late Bronze Age (750 B.C.) and the Iron Age (450–75 B.C.). Proficiency in spinning was increased by weighting spindles for twisting yarn, and upright looms were invented, in which the warp threads were held taut by means of clay weights, thus producing finer cloth. Roman civilization plus the Britons' native ingenuity produced a well-ordered province, although the inhabitants of the north and west were still primitive and barbaric. Julius Caesar observed that the natives of what are now the Midlands and North of England still wore skins, and their standards of agriculture and domestic life were far below those of the south-east. With the fall of the Roman Empire, the Legions left Britain in A.D. 410 to the doubtful mercy of invading Picts, Scots, Danes, and the Teutonic Angles, Jutes, and Saxons, who conquered and settled in Britain from the 5th century onwards. The high standards of Roman domestic life perished, and the 'Dark Ages' descended, obscure until a recognizable pattern of Saxon life gradually emerged.

On **Page 11** the British man and woman wear their traditional garments with additions due to Roman influence; the man's practical hooded cloak or PAENULA had an important and long-lasting influence on costume. The point of the hood was subsequently lengthened to become the medieval LIRIPIPE (21). The woman's long tunic conceals a thin white linen under-tunic or SHIFT. Her head is covered by a fold of her rectangular cloak or PALLA.

The butcher wears a rough, loose tunic common to all workmen under Roman rule. His shoes are of a similar, but improved, style to those already in use. The magistrate wears a typical Roman TOGA PRAETEXTA of white wool instead of the linen more suitable to the Italian climate. It is bordered with purple, according to his rank, also denoting priests and freeborn children. His TUNICA has a purple border at the neck, indicating that he is of senatorial rank. Class distinction in dress, as prescribed by social status and financial means, is already apparent. The magistrate's sandals or CALIGA could have stout leather soles studded with nails, as worn by marching legionaries.

The boy, carrying his bronze toy horse, wears a sleeveless tunic. The matron, dressed in Roman style adapted for the British climate, wears a sleeveless TUNICA or STOLA over a long-sleeved UNDERSHIFT or SUBUCULA. Her mantle is rectangular, and her elaborate Roman hairstyle is kept up with carved bone pins.

Materials Linen, woollen cloth.   **Furs** British native wild animals.
Colours White, purple, red, blue, and green.

BRITISH

BUTCHER

ROMAN-
BRITISH
MATRON

SANDALS
(Caliga)

MAGISTRATE

BOY

3 The Saxons 460–1066

The Saxons, a Teutonic tribe, gave their name to the form of civilization in these islands prior to the Norman invasion. They were primarily occupied in farming and defending their land against invaders, although their military organization lacked unity, which made them an easy prey to the disciplined feudalism of the Normans. They were not a cultured people and consequently did not develop generally high standards of art, literature, architecture, and fashions in clothes. In fact, the main purpose of clothing was to keep its wearer warm, as their dwellings had reverted to being uncomfortable and cold compared with the vanished Roman standards of comfort and heating. Yet the Saxons were not entirely barbaric, and they achieved a notable standard in the ornamental gold embroidery used on the cloaks and tunics of more prosperous members of society, i.e. nobility and thanes; this became famous as 'English work'.

A characteristic feature of Saxon dress as illustrated on **Page 13** was the long, tight, wrinkled sleeve. This was simply a device to keep the hands warm, by pulling the surplus length down, as gloves had not yet been invented.

The Saxon man wears a concealed linen UNDER-TUNIC or JUSTAUCORPS (i.e. 'next to the body') which was knee-length, as is his OVER-TUNIC. His loose BREECHES are cross-gartered, and his voluminous square MANTLE is fastened with a brooch on the shoulder. The style of his woollen cap is the jelly-bag or Phrygian type, eventually adopted by 18th-century French Revolutionaries as their 'cap of liberty'. His shoes (this word is derived from the Teutonic word *schah*), resemble those of the Ancient Britons. It was customary for commoners to wear black shoes, as coloured and embroidered footwear was reserved for the nobility. Saxon men wore their fair hair shoulder-length; their moustaches were long, and their beards parted in the centre, a style known as the BIFID beard.

The woman wears a long, wrinkled-sleeved UNDER-TUNIC or KIRTLE beneath her OVER-TUNIC or GUNNA which has shorter sleeves. Her head is covered by a HEAD-RAIL, kept in place with a metal FILLET, of gold if the owner were sufficiently wealthy. The ploughman is dressed in a tunic of rough woollen cloth. His leather shoes are extended to cover his ankles. The peasant woman or serf's wife wears a long KIRTLE, and hooded cloak which may well have been the forerunner of the WIMPLE(15).

Details of Saxon dress appear in the Bayeux tapestry.

Materials Rough woollens and linen.
Furs Nobility: Ermine and grey squirrel.
Freemen: Fox, marten, otter, and musk-rat.
Serfs: Rabbit, cat, and sheepskin.
Predominating colours Brown, green, and Prussian blue.

SAXONS

PLOUGHMAN   PEASANT WOMAN

4 The Normans 1066–1154

The Bayeux tapestry shows details of Early Norman dress. The clothes of Norman nobles were longer and more elaborate than those of the Saxons, who had to perform manual labour. Although Norman-French terms were introduced, no drastic revolution affected poorer folk's dress in 1066. Serfs still wore hoods, tunics, cross-gartered trousers, and leather shoes; these are not, therefore, shown in the Norman period.

The Norman gentleman on **Page 15** wears a long-sleeved linen UNDER-TUNIC or JUSTAUCORPS, nearly ankle-length, under a shorter-sleeved OVER-TUNIC, covered by a voluminous MANTLE fastened on the shoulder with a ring. On his legs are CHAUSSES or GAMACHES of linen, wool, or soft leather, tied by strings or tapes to the draw-string of short linen pants. Gradually more expertly cut, fitted and sewn CHAUSSES were the forerunners of modern stockings. Additional warm garments were cloaks, including a short HEUKE, a long, heavy SUPER-TOTUS, and an all-enveloping CHAPE. Men's hairdressing changed under William the Conqueror, who was reputed to have disliked the Saxons' flowing hair, moustaches, and beards, which returned to favour under William II.

Wealthy folk's shoes were of black or coloured embroidered leather; during William II's reign, they were becoming longer and more pointed, the toes being stuffed with wool. These 'piked' SABBATONS reached two inches beyond the natural foot by 1100. Serfs wore clumsy Saxon-type shoes or ankle-length boots. The lady wears a long-sleeved woollen or linen CHEMISE, CAMISE, or SHERTE; beneath her GOWN (a word derived from the Saxon *gunna*). Another type of GOWN was the BLIAUT, the bodice of which was laced at the sides to fit closely. Long, ornamental girdles were worn, and MANTLES were fastened over the chest with clasps and cord. A COUVRE-CHEF, like the Saxon HEAD-RAIL, covered long braided hair. A WIMPLE, covering throat and shoulders, could be added. After 1135 this signified a head-covering only, while a GORGET covered the throat. The Norman man-at-arms is protected by a HAUBERK of leather or stout linen reinforced with interlaced leather strips secured with metal studs, worn over a tunic. Its leather hood protects his head from the chafing of his conical helmet with its characteristic Norman nosepiece. The skirt of the HAUBERK was slit at the bottom for easy movement, not made into wide trouser-legs like the bowman's tunic; he wears a soft woollen or felt cap, in Saxon style, of any colour except yellow, worn only by Jews.

Materials Nobility: Wool, linen, *samite* (fine silk), *say* (worsted for *chausses*).
Peasants: Wool, linen, canvas, fustian.
Furs As for the Saxon period.
Colours Dull red, blue, green, and ochre-yellow.

NORMANS

CAP

SHOES

COUVRE-CHEF & WIMPLE

MAN-AT-ARMS BOWMAN

PEASANT'S HOOD

15

5 Medieval England

This period may be divided as follows: 1154-1272 The Plantagenets; 1272-1399 Early Gothic; 1399-1485 Gothic.

The Plantagenets

This was the age of the Crusades, which influenced English costume styles and, for those who could afford them, materials, notably the beautiful soft gay silks brought back from the East by returning Crusaders. However, the dress of the poorer members of the community was not affected, and they were not the target for Churchmen's furious denunciations against the growing extravagance of fashionable dress. Poorer folk continued to wear wool or linen.

The tradesman shown on **Page 17** wears a woollen tunic, woollen HOSE or CHAUSSES kept up by spiral bandages, a variation of cross-gartering. The increasingly pointed toes of shoes were stuffed with horsehair. The countrywoman wears a long GOWN and her head and shoulders are covered by a rectangular strip of material. The lawyer's undergarment is a linen SHERTE or CHEMISE. Over this he wears a long, tight-sleeved COTTE. Social status determined its length. Nobility, doctors, and lawyers were allowed to wear COTTES reaching to the ankles; those of merchants and traders reached mid-calf, while those of peasants reached the knees. The sleeves of the COTTE were usually cut in one piece with the body of the garment, in the style of the Eastern 'dalmatic', from which is derived the modern term dolman sleeves. Over his COTTE the lawyer wears a sleeveless SURCOTE or SURCOAT, adapted from the Crusaders' SURCOTE worn over armour. His hat, a high-crowned BYCOCKET, is of the type associated with Robin Hood.

The pilgrim or palmer, so called because those who had been to the Holy Land wore a sprig of palm in their hats, wears a COTTE covered by a camlet cloak, and a small shoulder-cape or PELERINE. The scallop shells adorning his hat show that he has been on pilgrimage to the shrine of St. James of Compostella. Those who had been to Rome wore crossed keys or leaden images of St. Peter. He carries the customary pilgrim's staff, with a large hook for his bundle, and a satchel or SCRIP. His hair and beard are long, as pilgrims usually let them grow untrimmed until they returned home. The peasant's rough tunic is slit down the sides below the waist. His trousers are cross-gartered and his rough leather shoes show little advance on Saxon footwear(13). The STARTUP or PERO (derived from the Roman term for a patrician's shoe) was a thonged leather boot worn by peasants performing wet and muddy work. The sole was studded with wooden pegs, like football boots, and afforded protection from the filthy mess of rotting bones, scraps, and rushes on floors. These pegged boots were a revival of the Roman fashion of reinforcing the soles of sandals with nails(11).

The peasant's COIF worn with or without a CHAPERON, was often adopted by the nobility when hunting, to protect their heads from overhanging

TRADES-
MAN

COUNTRY-
WOMAN

LAWYER

PEASANT

STARTUP or PERO

COIF

CHAPERON

PILGRIM

17

branches. The point of the CHAPERON or CAPUCHON was gradually becoming longer, to develop into the LIRIPIPE(21)

Gloves, often jewelled, were introduced during this period; naturally, only the rich could afford them, wearing them for hunting and hawking. Peasants wore rough woollen mittens.

Page 19 shows 13th-century styles. The townsman wears a thick, woollen, hooded travelling cloak or CAPA; the open armholes were evolved because of the unmanageable trailing sleeves worn by the nobility.

The lady wears a long COTTE with tight buttoned sleeves. Her MANTLE is fastened in the Norman fashion, and her GORGET is surmounted by a stiff linen cap or COIF; her unbound hair shows that she is unmarried. The servant has tucked up the skirt of her COTTE while doing wet or dirty work, thereby showing her KIRTLE underneath. A GORGET covers her neck, and her WIMPLE is knotted to keep it out of the way. The farmer's knee-length COTTE, is typical of the belted tunics worn by the working people for many years. His CHAPERON has a scalloped or DAGGED edge, a simplified version of the fanciful and decorative edging of Court dandies' garments known as SHATTERED, FLAMBOYANT, FOLIATED (cut into leaf shapes), and CASTELLATED (square-cut like battlements). He wears cloth HOSE and high leather boots.

The scholar is clothed in a calf-length COTTE under his GARDE-CORPS, a type of SURCOTE with hanging sleeves. His head is covered by a COIF.

The child's nurse wears a long COTTE under a voluminous PELISSE or PELICON, resembling the scholar's GARDE-CORPS. Her hooded CHAPERON is worn over a WIMPLE and GORGET.

The little girl wears a long-sleeved COTTE under a sleeveless indoor BLIAUT; her hair is kept in place by a FILLET.

Page 21 shows 14th-century costume.

The Jew, of about 1325, was obliged to wear a yellow cap. He wears a long-sleeved COTTE under a long robe or GABERDINE, later referred to by Shakespeare in *The Merchant of Venice*. His fur-trimmed cloak has open, hanging sleeves.

The merchant's wife, wearing a similar type of head-dress to the lady's on Page 19, is dressed in a long-sleeved COTTE under a sleeveless SURCOTE; the armholes fit normally, but Court ladies had the armholes of their SURCOTES and, later, their SUPER COTES-HARDIE cut so deeply that the front of the garment became a narrow strip. Shocked Churchmen called these large armholes 'windows of hell'. However, the modest and voluminous garments of citizens' wives were hardly likely to deserve such censure.

The farmer wears a short COTTE and cloth HOSE; his boots are slipped into wooden clogs or PATTENS, necessary for wet and muddy work. Over his hooded CHAPERON he wears a BYCOCKET hat. His hands are protected by rough woollen mitts.

The farm worker's long-sleeved COTTE, the skirt of which is horizontally striped, is displayed when the skirt of her SURCOTE is hitched up. Traces of this fashion still remain in the traditional dress of Scottish fisher girls. She wears a GORGET under her CHAPERON.

TOWNSMAN LADY SERVANT

NURSE

GIRL

FARMER SCHOLAR

19

By about 1325, the fashion of wearing garments in two colours was introduced, known as PARTI-COLOUR or MI-PARTI. The page is dressed in a short COTE-HARDIE, PARTI-COLOURED in the colours of his master's livery. The COTE-HARDIE fitted closely making a belt at the waist unnecessary. A low, ornamental belt was worn to carry a knife, dagger, or purse called an AUMONIÈRE or GIPCIÈRE. The point of the boy's CHAPERON has developed into a long LIRIPIPE. His pointed shoes echo the courtiers' fashion of wearing such extravagantly long pointed toes to their CRAKOWES that these had to be fastened to the knee with garters and gold chains. CRAKOWES were protected from muddy roads by pointed clogs or POULAINES. (Both terms are of Polish origin.)

The merchant, of about 1325, wears a longer version of the fitted COTE-HARDIE, with a low belt to carry his AUMONIÈRE or GIPCIÈRE. The hood and LIRIPIPE of his CHAPERON are thrown back. The peasant's tunic had not varied in style for hundreds of years; his loosely fitting breeches are draped from the side seams.

In 1363 strict Sumptuary Laws were passed, in an attempt to curb excesses in fashion during one of the most extravagant periods of English Costume. It was ordained that

1. The wearing of pearl embroidery and ermine be restricted to Royalty and nobility.
2. Cloth of gold, jewels, and linings of miniver fur could be worn only by knights and those of higher rank.
3. Cloth of silver, silver girdles, and fine quality wool might be worn only by squires and those of higher rank.
4. Commoners were allowed only coarser quality wool, silk and jewels being forbidden even if they could afford them.

Moreover, the length of CRAKOWES was limited as follows: nobility—24 inches beyond the natural foot; gentlemen—12 inches beyond the natural foot; commoners—6 inches beyond the natural foot.

Page 23 shows styles popular in the latter half of the 14th century.

Women continued to wear two dresses. The term COTTE was falling into disuse, the under-dress being known as the KIRTLE, which the citizen's wife wears with tight, buttoned sleeves under her GOWN, its pointed sleeves being a modest imitation of extravagant Court fashions. She wears a GORGET, and a stiff linen COIF. Following Court styles, her hair is neatly wound into net CAULS, which, if the owner were sufficiently wealthy or of good social status, were of gold thread.

This is the period of Chaucer's Canterbury Pilgrims, and some details of their dress are given in the *Prologue*.

'A good wyf was ther of bisydë Bathe . . .
Hir coverchiefs ful fynë were of ground;
I dorstë swere they weyëden ten pound,
That on a Sonday were upon hir heed.

JEW

MERCHANT'S WIFE

FARMER

FARM WORKER

PAGE

MERCHANT

PEASANT

21

Hir hosen weren of fyn scarlet reed,
Ful streite y-teyd, and shoes ful moyste and newe . . .
Y-wymplëd wel, and on hir heed an hat
As brood as is a bokeler or a targe;
A foot-mantel aboute hir hipës large,
And on hir feet a paire of sporës sharpe.'

The foot-mantle, not illustrated, was worn by ladies riding side-saddle, to protect them in bad weather.

'Ther was also a Nonne, a Prioresse . . .
Ful semëly hir wympel pinchëd was; . . .
Of smal coral aboute hir arm she bar
A peire of bedës gauded al with grene,
And ther-on heng a brooch of gold ful shene . . .'

'Pynched' meant pleated; the bib of her GORGET and WIMPLE was known also as the BARBE.

'A marchant was ther with a forkëd berd,
In mottëleye, and hye on horse he sat;
Upon his heed a Flaundrissh bever hat;
His bootës claspëd faire and fetisly. . . .'

The merchant has revived the Saxon BIFID beard(13); his motley dress is taken to mean brightly coloured cloth embroidered with flowers, made into a short belted HOUPPELANDE. This garment was a short version of the fashionable long, voluminous HOUPPELANDE, features of which were the high collar and set, padded pleats over the chest. The merchant's Flemish beaver hat is a BYCOCKET. 'With hym ther was a plowman. . . . In a tabard he rood upon a mere.'

His sleeveless TABARD is worn over a short COTTE.

'The revë was a sclendrë colerik man.
His berd was shave as ny as ever he can . . .
A long surcote of pers[1] upon he hade,
And by his syde he bar a rusty blade.'

Page 25 shows 15th-century fashions.

The architect, typical of prosperous professional men, wears a long, belted velvet HOUPPELANDE, with padded pleats and bag-sleeves as an alternative to wide, pointed ones. His hat is the fashionable ROUNDLET, which, with the similar but softer BERRETINO, had developed, with the addition of a stiffened brim, by fitting the face-opening of the CHAPERON on the top of the head, and twisting the surplus material into a fantastic coxcomb. The LIRIPIPE was lengthened into a long streamer, worn draped round the shoulders.

The merchant is dressed in an unbelted HOUPPELANDE typical of the reign of Henry IV (1399–1413); over the hood of his CHAPERON he wears a peaked, low-crowned BYCOCKET.

[1] Pers meant blue.

22

CITIZEN'S WIFE

WIF of BATHE

PRIORESSE

MARCHANT

PLOWMAN

REVE

23

The squire is fashionably attired in a short HOUPPELANDE and PARTI-COLOURED HOSE; because of the increasing brevity of the short HOUPPELANDE, HOSE were converted into nether-garments like modern tights, by the addition of the CODPIECE in front. The young man carries a SUGARLOAF or high BURGUNDIAN CAP, often of white felt. In his belt he carries a civilian dagger or ANELACE; knights carried MISERICORDES or daggers used to give the *coup de grâce* to fallen enemies in battle. His hair is cut in the bowl-crop style, adopted during Henry V's reign (1413–22).

The townswoman's HOUPPELANDE has bag-sleeves; her head is covered by a WIMPLE. The serving wench wears an apron, BARME-CLOTH or NAPRON over her GOWN. Her head-dress is adapted from the HENNIN, fashionable during the late 15th century. To a hood is added a black velvet FRONTLET framing the face, and a loop on the forehead, originally designed to stop a tall HENNIN from sliding backwards.

The tirewoman is dressed in a full-skirted GOWN. She wears a STEEPLE HENNIN, and GORGET.

The carpenter wears a skirted DOUBLET, and a hat with castellated brim, slowly developing into the Tudor style. His buttoned shoes, show the intermediate stage between 15th-century pointed CRAKOWES and 16th-century broad-toed SABETYNES.

Plantagenet Period

Materials	Wool, linen, and velvet.	Sarcinet or sarsanet (thin silk).
	Gauze (for veils and wimples).	Cendal (silk for lining cloaks).
	Burnet (brown cloth).	Bysine (made from flax).
	Camlet (wool and camel-hair for cloaks).	
	Ray (striped Flemish cloth).	
	Scarlet (soft woollen, dyed-in-the-yarn with cochineal, used for warm underwear—hence 'red flannel').	
	Brocella (peasants' rough wool).	
	Burel (peasants' coarse brown cloth).	
	Byrrhus (peasants' thick woollen cloth).	
Furs	Nobility: Ermine, sable, miniver, and grey squirrel.	
	Commoners: Basil (sheepskin), badger, musk-rat, and cat.	
Colours	Gay, jewel-like colours were worn by nobility and gentry, while poorer commoners wore dull, home-dyed brown, green, blue, grey, orange, and yellow.	

Early Gothic Period

Materials As for previous period, plus taffeta (mentioned by Chaucer).
Furs As for previous period, plus marten, fox, and rabbit for commoners.
Colours As for previous period.

Gothic

Materials, furs (plus beaver and otter for commoners) and **colours** as for previous periods.
There were many beautiful silks woven with gold and silver thread imported from the East, from the Plantagenet period onwards, but they have not been listed as they were not applicable to commoners.

ARCHITECT

MERCHANT

SQUIRE

CARPENTER

SERVING
WENCH

TOWNSWOMAN

TIREWOMAN

25

6 The Tudors 1485–1603

The end of the 15th century marked the end of the Middle Ages. The Renaissance brought tremendous advances in learning, painting, printing, and overseas exploration. Social conditions affected the costume of the period; the barrier between serfs and nobility during feudal and medieval times was gradually breaking down and a 'middle class' slowly emerged, due to the following reasons:

1. The increase in voyages of exploration encouraged trade. In 1600 Elizabeth I granted a charter to the East India Company. Merchants had become prosperous, building small town houses, living in style, and dressing well, if not as extravagantly as the Court.
2. The goldsmiths of the City of London were evolving a system of banking.
3. Since the Black Death in 1349, agricultural serfs and villeins were few; consequently Lords of the Manor had let out farm land for rent to a gradually emerging class of yeoman farmers. John Stephens wrote of a typical farmer in his *Essayes and Characters*: 'Doubtless he would murmur against the Tribune's law, by which none might occupy more than five hundred acres. . . . He is quickly and contentedly put into the fashion if his clothes be made against Whitsuntide or Christmas day.'

Since early medieval times outcries had been raised against the sin of extravagance in dress. In his *Description of England* (1587) William Harrison wrote angrily 'The fantastical folly of our nation (even from the courtier to the carter), is such that no form of apparel liketh us longer than the first garment is in the wearing, if it continue so long, and be not laid aside to receive some other trinket newly devised by the fickle-headed tailors, who covet to have several tricks in cutting thereby to draw fond customers to more expense of money.' Fynes Moryson commented in his *Itinerary*: 'All manners of attire came first into the city and country from the court, which, being once received by the common people, and by very stage-players themselves, the courtiers justly cast off, and take new fashions.'

In 1592 Thomas Nashe harshly criticized 'Mistress Minx, a merchant's wife', in his *Pierce Penilesse*. He stated that she spent 'half a day in pranking herself if she be invited to any strange place'.

Although these contemporary writers aver that commoners were striving to copy the nobility in fashion and extravagance, Sumptuary Laws, as summarized at the end of this chapter, were still in force.

The traditional figures on playing-cards date from the early years of this period.

Page 27 shows prevailing styles from 1485 to 1509.

The farmer is neither fashionable nor wealthy; he wears a shirt, which

COUNTRYMAN

BOY 1509

FARMER

COUNTRY-WOMAN

MARKET WOMAN

27

was now becoming an important garment for show, instead of a mere item of underclothes. The neck was gathered into a narrow band. Over this he wears a belted DOUBLET; his cloth HOSE are badly fitting, and his black cloth cap is an early form of Tudor head-dress. His shoes, no longer pointed, are in the Tudor broad-toed style.

The countryman is dressed in a DOUBLET, the ancestor of the traditional SMOCK(69). He wears loose cloth hose under an early type of BIGGENS or gaiters. The small boy, of a prosperous family, is clothed in a shirt under a skirted DOUBLET trimmed with black velvet at neck and hem. The countrywoman shows the back-laced bodice popular during this period; backlacing had been a medieval fashion. Her CHEMISE is similar in style to a man's shirt. The hemlines of the long, full skirts were usually trimmed with one or more bands of braid or velvet, depending on what the owner could afford. Women covered their heads with caps or COIFS. Under Sumptuary Laws, citizens' wives were obliged to wear COIFS of white woollen material unless their husbands could prove themselves gentlemen by descent, in which case, coifs were made of fine linen. The market woman protects her head with a simple strip of material.

Page 29 shows styles of costume worn up to about 1540.

The merchant wears a plain shirt, those of the nobility being finely embroidered at the neck in black and red; the next garment is a waist-length STOMACHER which may be considered as an early form of waistcoat. To this were fastened his long HOSE, laced with POINTS. Over the STOMACHER comes his knee-length DOUBLET, belted at the waist and pleated in the skirt. His outer garment is a LONG GOWN edged with fur; ermine and miniver were not allowed for commoners. The hanging sleeves are reminiscent of 13th-century fashions(19). His square cap is in the style generally worn by the nobility; his shoes are in the intermediate stage between medieval CRAKOWES and Tudor SABETYNES, which were known also as DUCK-BILLED, BUN-TOED, COW-MOUTHED, or BEAR-PAWED shoes. His garments are not ornamented with SLASHING, as this was forbidden for commoners by Sumptuary Laws. The chamberer or domestic servant has the sleeves of her GOWN rolled up for work, as short sleeves were not worn until the 17th century.

The merchant's wife wears an OVER-GOWN with a wide square neck showing the gathered PARTLET or GUIMPE, presumably the neck of her CHEMISE. Her patterned UNDER-GOWN or KIRTLE is displayed; round her shoulders she wears a long strip of warm material as a type of shawl, passed under the arms and tied round the waist. For indoor wear her cap or COIF is sufficient; for outdoor wear it is covered by the GABLE, KENNEL, or PEDIMENTAL head-dress shown below. This was made up as follows:

1. A white COIF.
2. A black veil covering the head and shoulders.
3. A stiff FRONTLET peaked in the centre, framing the face; this doubtless was derived from the 16th-century HENNIN(25).

MERCHANT'S WIFE
1538

CHAMBERER

MERCHANT

GABLE, KENNEL, or
PEDIMENTAL HEAD-DRESS

BURGESS

HEAD-DRESS
WORN BY
SPINSTER

SABETYNE

The head-dress worn by the spinster is very similar to that worn by the servant on Page 19. A spinster did not then signify an 'old maid', but a spinning-woman. The SABETYNE shows how SLASHING was used on shoes; this was not applicable to commoners.

The burgess wears the type of cap generally worn by clergy, scholars, and lawyers. His curiously hooded LONG GOWN has very full sleeves.

Page 31 shows styles worn from 1540 onwards.

The citizen's wife, of about 1560, wears a full-skirted GOWN with padded SHOULDER-WINGS, a typical Elizabethan fashion. She is holding a POKING-STICK used for re-setting RUFFS after washing and starching; this tool is mentioned by Shakespeare in *The Winter's Tale* when Autolycus the pedlar sings of 'Pins and poking-sticks of steel'.

The schoolmaster is dressed in a LONG GOWN with medieval hanging sleeves (19). His loose, baggy breeches were called SPANISH SLOPS. He wears a small RUFF as a collar. The student's LONG GOWN is the forerunner of present-day university gowns. He also wears a RUFF. The apprentice of 1550 wears a blue calf-length GOWN over white breeches and yellow HOSE. The uniform still worn by the boys of Christ's Hospital is based on this. His head-dress is a flat MARIAN CAP, and he wears a plain turn-down collar. The apprentice of 1580–90 is dressed in a belted DOUBLET and ROUND or MELON HOSE.

Apprentices' clothing was subject to strict 'Regulations recommended for the Apparel of London Apprentices' published by the Lord Mayor and Common Council in 1582, which ruled that from thenceforth no Apprentice whatsoever should presume to wear any apparel but what he receives from his Master; to wear no hat within the City and liberty thereof, nor anything instead thereof, but a woollen cap, without any silk in or about the same; to wear no ruffles, cuffs, loose collar, nor other thing than a ruff at the collar, and that only of a yard and a half long; to wear no doublets, but what were made of canvas, fustian, sackcloth, English leather, or woollen cloth, and without being enriched with any manner of gold, silver, or silk; to wear no other coloured cloth or kersey[1] in hose or stocking, than white, blue, or russet; to wear little breeches of the same stuffs as the doublets, and without being stitched, laced, or bordered; to wear a plain upper coat of cloth or leather without pinking, stitching, edging, or silk about it; to wear no other surcote than a cloth gown or cloak, lined or faced with cloth, cotton, or bays, with a fixed round collar without stitching, garding,[2] lace, or silk; to wear no pumps, slippers nor shoes but of English leather, without being pinked, edged, or stitched, nor girdles, nor garters, other than of crewel, woollen thread, or leather, without being garnished; to wear no sword, dagger, or other weapon but a knife; nor a ring, jewel of gold nor silver, nor silk in any part of his apparel.

[1] Course ribbed woollen cloth.
[2] Seams covered by braid.

CITIZEN'S
WIFE

SCHOOLMASTER

STUDENT

MERCHANT

APPRENTICES
1550   1580-90

31

The illustrations on **Page 33** show the typical styles of dress worn during the latter half of the 16th century, the Elizabethan period.

The merchant wears a DOUBLET, based on the padded PEASECOD DOUBLET made fashionable by wealthier folk; his breeches are short TRUNKHOSE worn over long HOSE or NETHERSTOCKS. His knee-length boots are of soft leather. Heels on boots and shoes appeared about 1602. His short cloak, bordered with braid, is in the Spanish style, made popular by the marriage of Mary Tudor and Philip of Spain. He wears a SUIT OF RUFFS at neck and wrists, but these do not reach the immense proportions of those worn at Court.

The doctor wears a LONG GOWN, a customary garment of professional men. His flat MARIAN CAP is worn over a COIF, and he carries a bag of philtres and potions with a scroll of prescriptions fitted at the base.

The gown of the citizen's wife shows the characteristic padded SHOULDER-WINGS of this period and two rows of braid at the hem. Her collar follows the fashion of the WHISK, a wide stiffened collar, as worn by Shakespeare in the Chandos portrait; this gradually replaced RUFFS. The quality of her cap or COIF depended on her social status. The market woman wears a MUFFLER to protect her mouth from cold or infection. Over a COIF she wears a THRUMMED hat, i.e. of long-haired felt. These two items are mentioned by Shakespeare in *The Merry Wives of Windsor* when Falstaff was attempting to disguise himself as 'the Fat Woman of Brentford': 'Mistress Page: And there's her thrummed hat and her muffler too.'

An early method of making felt was to damp wool fibres and then to beat them hard with heavy sticks.

The pedlar wears DOUBLET and knee-breeches with woollen HOSE, often white. His square-toed shoes have heels, and he wears the popular MARIAN CAP. Pedlars carried a varied stock of fairings for sale, as listed by Shakespeare in *The Winter's Tale* in the song of Autolycus:

> 'Lawn as white as driven snow,
> Cyprus black as e'er was crow,
> Gloves as sweet as damask roses,
> Masks for faces and for noses;
> Bugle bracelet, necklace amber,
> Perfume for a lady's chamber;
> Golden quoifs, and stomachers
> For my lads to give their dears;
> Pins and poking-sticks of steel,
> What maids lack from head to heel . . .'

CYPRUS was a soft, fine silk often dyed black and used for veiling. QUOIFS were netted COIFS or CAULS (23). Pins and steel needles, hitherto imported from France were made in England during this period, and were expensive; hence the need for 'pin-money'.

The farm hand wears loose, baggy breeches or SPANISH SLOPS with coarse woollen HOSE and ankle-length boots.

MERCHANT 1590

DOCTOR

CITIZEN'S WIFE 1600

MARKET WOMAN

PEDLAR 1602

FARM HAND

Page 35 shows Elizabethan fashions up to 1600.

The farm hand wears a short-sleeved DOUBLET over his shirt: this could have been the ancestor of the smock (69). His HOSE are of coarse wool, and his hat of rough felt. The prosperous farmer wears a loose DOUBLET (also a forerunner of the smock) over his ruffed shirt and full, short TRUNKHOSE. His hat is based on the fashionable COPOTAIN worn by nobility.

The peasant wears a loose belted DOUBLET over loose, ill-fitting HOSE. His hat is of coarse felt. The vagabond wears ragged versions of the items of clothing in general use.

The small boy is a page in a gentleman's service, and wears a padded DOUBLET with the usual SHOULDER-WINGS; his breeches are baggy SPANISH SLOPS.

The domestic servant has pinned up the skirt of her GOWN while she is doing wet or dirty work, thus showing her KIRTLE or petticoat. Her sleeves are rolled up, for, until the early 17th century, long sleeves were universally worn and bare arms were never shown. She is old fashioned as she wears, for warmth, a GORGET (19) with a COIF under her THRUMMED hat.

The citizen's daughter wears a pinafore or FORESMOCK over her GOWN, which has a small plain collar and cuffs.

Page 37 shows Late Elizabethan fashions at the turn of the century.

The gentleman's wife is wearing an elaborate dress with quilted STOMACHER and KIRTLE, the skirt being held out by a French type DRUM-SHAPED FARTHINGALE. Her waist is encircled by a box-pleated WAIST-RUFF; the long, tapering effect of her bodice was achieved by means of rigid corsets or BODY-STICHET, made of strips of wood and canvas, worn under a stiff STOMACHER. In lieu of a RUFF she wears a high WHISK of lace-edged lawn, with matching cuffs.

The scholar wears a LONG GOWN with embroidered SHOULDER-WINGS and hanging sleeves; this garment was commonly worn by elderly statesmen and professional men. His head is covered by a flat MARIAN CAP, a modern survival of which is worn by Knights of the Garter and Yeoman Warders at the Tower of London. Note his shoes; heels were not generally worn until about 1602. He wears moderately sized RUFFS at neck and wrists.

FARMER

PEASANT

FARM HAND

VAGABOND

PAGE

SERVANT

CITIZEN'S DAUGHTER

ROUND or MELON HOSE were an adaptation of padded TRUNKHOSE and were usually worn over long HOSE without CANIONS or UPPERSTOCKS illustrated on Page 39.

Cork-soled MULES or PANTOFFLES were worn as indoor slippers. The style of FRENCH HOOD shown is associated with Mary Queen of Scots from about 1580 onwards.

Page 39 illustrates Late Elizabethan fashions up to 1602.

The gentleman wears a tightly fitting PEASECOD DOUBLET, although this is not extravagantly padded and peaked in the style of Court dandies. His short, padded TRUNKHOSE are worn over long HOSE, the upper part of his legs being covered by closely fitting CANIONS or UPPERSTOCKS, the lower part by NETHERSTOCKS. His RUFF is of modest proportions, unlike the enormous MILLSTONE RUFFS favoured at Court. His hat is a stiff-crowned COPOTAIN trimmed with a small plume. Note that his shoes and those of his children have heels.

The small boy wears a closely fitting DOUBLET with SHOULDER-WINGS typical of this period, and unpadded breeches or VENETIANS. His soft, turn-down, lace-edged collar is a variation from the stiff RUFF and a forecast of Stuart fashions of the subsequent period.

The girl's full-skirted dress has padded SHOULDER-WINGS or EPAULETS; her RUFF is soft and unstarched, and her closely fitting cap is embroidered. The linen stocking, stitched in colour and laced at the ankle (the origin of clocks on more modern stockings and socks), was generally worn until the invention of the stocking-frame in 1589, when knitted stockings were introduced. Queen Elizabeth I is said to have been delighted with her first pair of black silk. Subsequently, less expensive cotton stockings were known as CALABER WEB HOSE.

Heels on shoes quickly became popular and higher; toes were squared off and slightly turned up. High cork CHOPINES, a refined form of clogs, were worn both as a protection from muddy roads and to make the wearer look taller.

An alternative to the RUFF was the WHISK, as worn by Shakespeare; this was made of starched linen, lawn, or lace, and kept up by REBATOS which were strips of pasteboard covered with silk or satin.

GENTLEMAN'S WIFE

SCHOLAR

ROUND or MELON HOSE

FRENCH HOOD

MULES or PANTOFFLES

Summary of commoners' and peasants' clothes (as prescribed by Sumptuary Laws)

Doublets and breeches Plain woollen cloth (no slashing).
Shirts Unbleached linen with narrow, plain collars.
Hose Wool, often white.
Shoes Leather; low heels after 1602.
Gowns Servants' gowns might reach the calf of the leg, but no longer.
Caps Citizens' wives must wear caps of white woollen yarn, unless their husbands could prove themselves gentlemen by descent.
Hats Flat Marian caps.

Materials used by commoners

Bays or *bayze*	Flemish wool.
Boulters	Open-mesh woollen.
Callimancoes	Glazed camel-hair and wool.
Carrells	Silk and worsted.
Harden	Coarse hemp or flax.
Nettlecloth	Rough wool.
Pampilion	Cloth for liveries.
Sammeron	Linen.
Say or *saye*	Coarse Flemish wool.
Shag	Rough, hairy wool and camel-hair.
Stammel or *estamel*	Coarse red cloth.

Predominating colours of commoners' clothes

Women's woollen GOWNS and KIRTLES were usually of dull colours i.e. grey, russet, and black.

GENTLEMAN *and* FAMILY 1602

LINEN STOCKING

LADY'S SHOE 1602

WHISK

CORK CHOPINE

7 The Stuarts 1603–1714

Like the Tudor sovereigns, James I had great personal influence on styles of dress. He is reputed to have been in such constant and cowardly fear of assassination by stabbing or shooting that he favoured BOMBASTED BREECHES and DOUBLETS, that is, garments heavily padded with wool, horsehair, or sawdust. National events during this period—the Civil War, Commonwealth, and Restoration—certainly had a profound effect on costume.

The gentleman on **Page 41** is wearing BOMBASTED BREECHES and DOUBLET; his SUIT OF RUFFS at neck and wrists is of small proportions. The ornament on his shoes is a revival of an Early Tudor fashion of SLASHING the outer material of a garment to show a gay lining. Up to 1616 the wide and unwieldy DRUM-SHAPED or CARTWHEEL FARTHINGALE was still worn by women (37). As this style took up a vast amount of room at Court functions, James I decreed that it should no longer be worn; it therefore went out of fashion, and softer, unstiffened skirts were worn, as by the lady of 1617, whose high, lace-edged WHISK necessitated a high, upswept hairstyle, called ARCELETS. The GOLILLA, a small stiff collar, probably originated from the stiffened UNDERPROPPER worn to keep up the enormously wide MILL-STONE RUFFS of the Elizabethan period.

The boy wears a full-sleeved DOUBLET and baggy, unpadded breeches called GALLIGASKINS.

The FALLING RUFF was merely an unstarched version of that worn in the preceding period. Note the small beard and LIP-TUFT favoured by this man and also the gentleman of 1605.

GENTLEMAN
1605

LADY
1617

BOY
1625

GOLILLA
1623

FALLING RUFF
1625

41

On **Page 43** the schoolmaster is dressed in DOUBLET and baggy GALLI-
GASKINS under his academic GOWN; his collar is a FALLING RUFF. The
townswoman wears a GOWN with a full, unstiffened skirt. Her wide, lace-
edged collar is typical of the period and more elaborate and exquisite
examples may be seen in portraits of the time, painted by Van Dyck.
The boy is clothed in DOUBLET with lace collar, and fairly narrow
GALLIGASKINS; he carries a wide-brimmed Cavalier-style hat. Shoes were
generally adorned with rosettes. Red heels were a mark of rank and
nobility. The little girl wears a GOWN similar in cut and style to the
dresses worn by grown-ups. Children's clothes continued to be miniature
copies of those of their elders, until 1770, when juvenile fashions were
created for them, as may be seen in Gainsborough's paintings. Note the
length of her sleeves; until this period sleeves were always long.

Small embroidered caps were sometimes worn by children, although
fashionable women were usually bareheaded indoors.

SCHOOLMASTER
1630

TOWNSWOMAN 1630

BOY
1630

GIRL
1635

GIRL'S CAP 1635

43

On **Page 45** the countryman wears, over his linen shirt and woollen breeches, a sleeveless JERKIN which could be made of coarse wool or leather. Shoes were now trimmed with heavy buckles of steel for poorer folk, and of silver for those able to afford it.

The countrywoman's clothes foreshadow Puritan styles(47). Her wide linen collar is a plain, unadorned version of the Van Dyck style(43). Contrary to the bareheaded fashion of townswomen, countrywomen were more conservative and continued to wear linen caps.

With the adoption of lower necklines to dresses and as high RUFFS and WHISKS were no longer worn, a longer hairstyle with ringlets became popular; this also featured a high, coiled chignon and a curly BULL'S HEAD FRINGE or TAURE.

Royalist Cavaliers of this period sometimes wore TUBULAR BREECHES fringed at the knees with ribbon loops. Riding-boots became increasingly important; they could be either very low BUCKET-TOPPED, soft and wrinkled and of moderate length(47), or very high and deeply cuffed. All these styles had heavy STIRRUP-LEATHERS over the instep. As heavy boots quickly wore out expensive silk stockings, BOOT HOSE were made of hard-wearing material such as linen, with deep lace cuffs or FRENCH FALLS.

Men's hairstyles grew to shoulder-length, and Cavaliers wore small, pointed Van Dyck beards.

COUNTRYMAN
1635

COUNTRYWOMAN
1638

HAIRSTYLE
1640

TUBULAR
BREECHES

BOOT HOSE

HAIRSTYLE
1642

BUCKET BOOTS 1645

45

Page 47 illustrates styles of dress worn by the opposing factions in the Civil War. The Cavalier wears a SHORT-WAISTED DOUBLET adorned with a Van Dyck collar; his breeches are GALLIGASKINS, GALLEYHOSEN, or SLOPS, worn with soft boots and BOOT HOSE. The popularity of lace for those who could afford it is shown in the illustration of the Cavalier's small daughter. Her mother wears a GOWN trimmed at the waist with tabs or PICCADILS. The sleeves are of the fashionable shorter length, and the skirt is fastened back to show the KIRTLE or PETTICOAT. Her hairstyle is shown on Page 45.

Clothes of both men and women of Royalist sympathies were made of soft, pastel-coloured satin rather than the stiff, heavy brocades of preceding periods—worn, naturally, only by those who could afford them. But now the quality and fineness of materials were governed by consideration of expense, rather than by the Sumptuary Laws passed in previous reigns.

Gay clothes were frowned upon by the ardent supporters of Cromwell, known as Puritans or Roundheads, who did not evolve new fashions but made existing styles plain, unadorned, and dull in colour, mostly black, brown, and soft grey. Men's hair was cropped; hats were high and STEEPLE-CROWNED, those of the women being worn over white caps which completely covered the hair. These hats are the origin of those worn with the modern (not ancient) version of Welsh national costume. Both Puritan men and women wore plain linen collars and cuffs. Roundhead soldiers have been included, as many men were in uniform during the Civil War; the trooper of 1648 wears a buff leather JERKIN over his DOUBLET. His head is protected by a LOBSTER-TAILED HELMET. The halberdier is wearing a steel breastplate or CUIRASS over his DOUBLET, which has the customary linen collar; his breeches are very full. His helmet is of the type known as a COMB MORION. This uniform is still worn by members of the Honourable Artillery Company.

The general jubilation at the Restoration of King Charles II in 1660 had a marked effect on the costume of the period. After the restraints of the Commonwealth, men's fashions in particular became extravagant and, indeed, ridiculous.

CAVALIER and FAMILY
1645

PURITANS
1645

ROUNDHEAD
1648

HALBERDIER 1648

47

The townsman on **Page 49** wears a moderate version of PETTICOAT or RHINEGRAVE BREECHES, the popularity of which lasted only until about 1680. This style was introduced into France by the Rhinegrave of Salm. Under a short bolero-type DOUBLET fashionable men wore a voluminous shirt trimmed at the neck with FALLING BANDS. The PETTICOAT BREECHES illustrated are adorned at the waist with loops of ribbon. It was not uncommon for a wealthy Restoration dandy's outfit to be trimmed with 140 yards of silk ribbon! The townsman wears full knee-breeches beneath his petticoat. His square-toed shoes are trimmed with wired ribbon butterfly-bows which were replacing metal buckles. His hat is the shallow broad-brimmed style normally worn by the middle class; this could have been the foundation of the TRICORNE commonly worn during the 18th century.

Long hair returned to favour, and servants grew their natural hair to this style; the majority of other men, however, wore long, curly PERIWIGS; unless naturally bald, their own hair was shaved off or cut very short, nightcaps being worn when wigs were taken off. It may well be that a contributory reason to the popularity of PERIWIGS was that many erstwhile Roundhead supporters hastily changed their allegiance at the Restoration, and thankfully covered their tell-tale cropped pates. Wigs made of human hair were very expensive, so that goat-hair and horsehair were used. Many illuminating remarks on fashion may be found in the *Diary* of Samuel Pepys, who wrote in 1665 that he was extremely chary of putting on his splendid new wig, as he strongly suspected that it had been made of hair obtained from recently dead victims of the Great Plague.

Men sometimes carried MUFFS, also called SNOSKYNS or SNUFFKINS. Pepys borrowed one from his wife.

In view of the expanse of shirt, it is regrettable that it was often dirty, as the frequent washing of clothes or body was not a fashionable habit; strong perfume was used.

Ladies' hairstyles became more luxuriant and coquettish. Necklines of dresses descended, and detachable gathered sleeves were popular. Laced corsets were worn to give a slender, smooth line to the peaked bodices of ladies' dresses. The corset illustrated has tabs or PICCADILS to ensure a snug fitting over the wearer's hips.

The lady of 1665 is fashionably dressed in her tight-bodiced, full-skirted GOWN over her KIRTLE, now being called a PETTICOAT. Her full sleeves are of the now customary elbow-length.

The Dutch jacket, seen in many of the paintings of Vermeer and other Dutch artists of the period, became popular in Great Britain. It was usually made of black velvet and trimmed with white fur.

TOWNSMAN 1660

HAIRSTYLE 1660

DETACHABLE SLEEVES

LADY 1665

CORSET

DUTCH JACKET

49

Page 51 illustrates types of garments worn by middle-class citizens during the reign of Charles II.

The townswoman wears a wadded waistcoat with tabs or PICCADILS at the waist; she is *en negligé*, the equivalent of a modern slattern's appearing in hair-curlers and dressing-gown. A woman's first and innermost garment was a long SHIFT of fine HOLLAND (linen) or lawn under her corset. With the addition of a waistcoat and full skirt, and a KERCHIEF over her hair, the casual toilette is complete. The laced-up front view of the wadded waistcoat is also shown.

Feminine hairstyles became more *bouffant*, being copies of Nell Gwyn's curly locks; curls, called HEART-BREAKERS, were wired to stand away from the face. The elderly lady's travelling-hood is a direct descendant of the hoods worn in Roman Britain(11) and throughout succeeding centuries.

The manservant is dressed in a plain version of the CASAQUE, CASSOCK-COAT, or PERSIAN VEST, a fashion originating from Persia personally sponsored by Charles II in October 1666, and which replaced PETTICOAT BREECHES(49). Men of fashion wore under this coat a long waistcoat, adapted from the DOUBLET. Breeches were still baggy. Round his neck the servant wears a plain NECKCLOTH, which became known as GENEVA BANDS, later worn principally by clergymen, and in modern times by clergymen and barristers.

Further references to clothes in Pepys's *Diary* include his 'flowered tabby vest' and 'coloured camelott tunique', signifying his flowered watered-silk taffeta waistcoat and fine woollen coat. He stated that his wife refurbished a shabby dress by covering it with lace. She, and other women anxious to be stylish, added false hair to their own tresses.

TOWNSWOMAN
1670

HAIRSTYLE
1670

WADDED WAISTCOAT

TRAVELLING HOOD
1664

MANSERVANT 1670

51

Page 53 shows styles of garments worn during the reigns of Charles II, William III and Mary, and Queen Anne.

Nell Gwyn often wore gay dresses with low *décolletage* showing glimpses of chemise at shoulders and sleeves, trimmed with a suggestion of SLASHING. As already described, her curly hair was much copied.

The gentleman of 1680 is dressed in a full-skirted CASSOCK-COAT; breeches were becoming less baggy and known as CULOTTES. His PERIWIG is long and curly. Frills on the sleeves of his shirt always showed at his wrists.

The FONTANGE, TOWER, or COMMODE was a fashionable head-dress very popular during the reign of William and Mary. It is reputed to have been invented in France by a Mademoiselle de Fontange, who, in a mood of gay abandon while out hunting, tied up her curls with her garter trimmed with lace and ribbons. The head-dress became very tall and was tilted forward, showing front curls, and was kept in position by a small cap over the back of the head. Long streamers or LAPPETS hung over the shoulders. Frilled MOB CAPS, and present-day waitresses' caps developed from the FONTANGE.

Both men's and women's shoes were fastened with buckles again. After 1689, Queen Mary was largely responsible for the introduction and popularity of printed calicoes and chintzes, used as dress materials.

As worn by
NELL GWYNN
1670

GENTLEMAN
1680

MAN'S SHOE 1700

LADY'S SHOE 1700

FONTANGE, TOWER or COMMODE 1690

Page 55 illustrates styles worn during the reign of Queen Anne, up to 1714.

The butcher is dressed in a blue FROK, commonly worn by butchers and tallow-chandlers, with a wide-brimmed felt hat.

By 1714 the FONTANGE had decreased in height and was developing into the MOB CAP.

Long, elaborate PERIWIGS were not practical for men engaged in battles; therefore shorter CAMPAIGN WIGS were introduced for military use and passed into civilian fashion. One of these was the RAMILLIES WIG named after the battle in 1706; instead of curls at the nape of the neck it featured a neat plaited QUEUE tied with a black bow. Hair was powdered with edible wheat-flour. Wealthy folk had powder-rooms set aside for the purpose; during the operation their faces were covered with paper FACE CONES. Poorer folk powdered their hair outside their front doors. The STEINKIRK CRAVAT had been introduced in 1692; it was an accidental fashion, as soldiers at the Battle of Steinkirk, faced with a surprise attack, dressed in some confusion and hastily twisted their NECKCLOTHS or CRAVATS.

The dairymaid wears a laced bodice similar to modern peasant costume. Her head is covered by a KERCHIEF and black felt hat.

Materials Linen, lawn, and lace for collars and cuffs.
Pastel-coloured satins.
Sober-coloured woollens worn by Puritans.
Velvet.
Printed calicoes and chintzes—after 1689.

BUTCHER
1705

FONTANGE
1714

DAIRYMAID
1711

RAMILLIES
WIG
1706 *onwards*

STEINKIRK CRAVAT
1692 *onwards*

8 The Hanoverians 1714–1837

The 18th century, often called 'The Age of Elegance', was an age of style, beauty, wit, and sophisticated vice with the simultaneous contrast of squalor, poverty, and degradation; elaborate wigs and hooped skirts were commonly verminous and dirty, and much strong perfume was used. Again, international events had marked repercussions on fashion. For example, the French Revolution led to simpler styles, and the constant threat of war, entailing heavy national expenditure on naval and military forces, led to increased taxation; a tax on hair powder was imposed in 1796, which brought the powdering of hair and wigs to an abrupt end. National and social events also had their effect; the Industrial Revolution brought an end to colourful and elaborate fashions for men. It was no longer practical for them to wear gay silks, satins, and velvets among industrial smoke and dirt.

It was the age of many great painters, including Gainsborough, Morland, Raeburn, Reynolds, Romney, and Zoffany. Their paintings are a valuable and accurate record of the costume of the period.

The Georgian gentleman of 1720 on **Page 57** is wearing a coat or JUSTAUCORPS. (The skirts of such coats were stiffened with canvas or paper until about 1750.) His waistcoat is still long. Stockings were worn rolled over knee-breeches until about 1730, after which breeches or CULOTTES were buttoned or buckled at the knee. The gentleman carries a TRICORNE hat. His powdered PERIWIG is peaked high at the centre parting.

The country squire's wife is dressed with a careful and studied simplicity. The skirt of her GOWN is parted to display her flowered JUPE or petticoat. Her shoulders are covered with a FICHU, and over a small MOB CAP she wears a Leghorn straw hat. Open-work MITTENS were fashionable.

Hoods were still frequently worn, and red CARDINALS were smart; these were the origin of Red Riding Hood. Servants wore full MOB CAPS, not as small and stylish as those worn by ladies when indoors. The KEVENHULLER HAT was a form of the TRICORNE, worn with one peak in the centre and always trimmed with gold braid or GALLOON. By 1730 tie-wigs had replaced PERIWIGS.

1720

GENTLEMAN

COUNTRY SQUIRE'S
WIFE
1727

'CARDINAL' HOOD
1725

SERVANT'S
MOB CAP 1730

KEVENHULLER
HAT 1735

Page 59 illustrates Georgian fashions.

The gentleman of 1735 wears a full-skirted, double-breasted overcoat over his striped silk JUSTAUCORPS. His breeches are buttoned at the knee, and his variation of the TIE-WIG is a BAG-WIG, the QUEUE or back-curls being enclosed in a black bag to keep powder off the coat collar.

The lady of 1735 is dressed in a SACK-BACKED GOWN which had been developed from the loose, comfortable French CONTOUCHE. This style may be seen in the paintings of Watteau, and remained in fashion until about 1785. The pleats of the back panel of the dress were called WATTEAU PLEATS. The voluminous skirt is held out over wicker PANIERS or hoops. It should be noted that the term PANIER correctly refers to the framework supporting skirts and not to the puffs of material over the hips; these were known as the POLONAISE. The lady's head is covered by a small MOB CAP or DEMI-BONNET known as the CLOSE JOAN.

The MOB CAP was adapted to various styles, as shown.

GENTLEMAN
1735

LADY
1735

1736

1740

1740

TYPES of MOB CAP

59

Page 61 shows that the general line and style of clothes worn by members of the working classes did not vary for many years. The cook is wearing the GOWN, apron or PINNER, and MOB CAP, typical garments worn by servants of the period and after.

The farm hand is dressed in shirt, knee-breeches, and stout woollen stockings.

The BOB WIG is of the type associated with Dr. Johnson. Up to the closing years of the century, wigs were powdered white or grey. Other styles included the BRUTUS, HEDGEHOG (shaggy all over), COMET, CAULIFLOWER, and GRIZZLE MAJOR, besides the extraordinary models affected by the dandies of the time.

The enormously high and ornamented coiffures worn by wealthy and fashionable ladies in the 1770s and 1780s were beyond the means of middle-class women and utterly impractical for those engaged in manual work. However, women did what they could and piled their hair as high as was possible, keeping it tidy with small lace-trimmed caps, as shown.

Another variation of the MOB CAP is illustrated.

COOK
1745

FARM HAND
1750

BOB WIG
1760

CAP 1765

CAP
1765

61

The WATERMAN shown on **Page 63** is dressed in garments similar to the traditional costume worn by Thames watermen of today, the holders of the Doggett's Coat and Badge. His coat or JUSTAUCORPS is very full skirted.

The servant wears the customary full-skirted GOWN, with a large FICHU crossed and tied round the waist. Her cap is not frilled, being of use rather than ornament.

The TRICORNE hat is plain and untrimmed with braid, and is of the type usually worn by working men, such as sedan-chair bearers and linkmen. This man wears his own hair, not a wig.

The carter wears a long waistcoat and a high-crowned black hat which is reminiscent of Puritan styles (47).

The Leghorn 'Shepherdess' hat, a countrywomen's style, was adopted by fashion-conscious townswomen anxious to maintain an appearance of artless simplicity in the 'Dolly Varden' manner. Wide straw hats are seen in many Gainsborough portraits.

Long-distance journeys by 18th-century stage-coaches were hazardous both because of highwaymen and inclement weather; consequently, men and women were warmly wrapped in voluminous travelling-cloaks or coats.

WATERMAN
1765

SERVANT
1770

CARTER
1775

TRICORNE HAT
1780

LEGHORN HAT 1785

The lady of 1790 on **Page 65** is dressed in a heavy woollen caped cloak with armhole slits. She wears a tall hat, based on men's styles, tall because hairstyles were still high and *bouffant*.

Her companion wears a caped overcoat fastened with buttoned tabs, and heavy riding-boots. From this time onward, riding-boots were trimmed with yellow turn-down cuffs at the knees and were called JOCKEY BOOTS. As an alternative to the TRICORNE hat he wears a high-crowned BEAVER hat.

Another type of hat fashionable during this period was the BICORNE, so called because the broad brim was peaked into two points instead of the three of the TRICORNE. This style is usually associated with Lord Nelson and Napoleon, and was technically described as being cocked *à l'Androsmane*. It seems to have been a popular fashion with leading French Revolutionaries.

Closely fitting gaiters or SPATTERDASHES were commonly worn by military and civilian men as a protection from mud; long after they went out of fashion they were retained by agricultural workers(69), and are still worn in modern times by Anglican Church dignitaries.

Styles of ladies' bonnets were many and various. The model of 1800 shown was based on the shape of some classical helmets.

By 1800 knee-breeches were no longer fashionable, except for Court and ambassadors' dress. This change was largely due to the French Revolution, during which types of garments associated with the aristocrats were vigorously discouraged.

TRAVELLING CLOTHES

1790

1795

BICORNE HAT

SPATTERDASHES
1800

1790

BONNET
1800

As shown on **Page 67**, the gentleman of 1805 wears tightly fitting PANTALOONS, made of a springy, stretchable fabric called KERSEYMERE, to ensure that they fitted as closely as possible. Dandies actually damped the fabric in order to obtain a perfect fit. The modern centre-front fastening of men's trousers had not yet been introduced; they were still fastened by a two- or three-buttoned flap called *à pont*. This gentleman's coat is cut away at the front, leaving a trace of the skirt of the garment, as worn during the preceding period, in the two coat-tails. This fashion is still preserved in modern evening dress. The BEAVER hat shown was currently fashionable.

Between 1800 and 1816 Beau Brummel was supreme in the world of men's fashion. While his immediate circle included the Prince Regent and Court dandies (Corinthians, Smarts, and Fribbles), he had a profound influence on the supremacy of English tailoring and on personal cleanliness, insisting that the smell of freshly laundered linen was preferable to that of lavishly applied perfume.

The lady of 1807, familiar in style from illustrations and dramatizations of the novels of Jane Austen, wears an Empire style dress. These straight, high-waisted gowns were introduced during the closing years of the 18th century and were a swift and extreme change from the wide hooped skirts of the previous period. Her shoes are a complete change from high-heeled, buckled shoes to flat pumps, introduced at the time of the French Revolution. She carries a RETICULE, a netted handbag originated during the French Directoire period.

The blacksmith's shirt, knee-breeches, and coarse woollen stockings may be taken as typical of working men's dress for many years. Knee-breeches were retained by them for practical reasons regardless of fashion.

Another fashionable style of bonnet is shown, as worn in 1805. The elderly countrywoman wears a voluminous cloak, and closely fitting indoor cap. The soft-crowned hat of 1815, an alternative to the bonnet, is reminiscent of the Elizabethan COPOTAIN(39).

GENTLEMAN
1805

LADY
1807

BLACKSMITH
1810

BONNET
1805

1810
COUNTRYWOMAN

HAT
1815

Page 69 illustrates types of garments worn by agricultural workers during the early years of the 19th century.

The farm hand wears a linen smock, often considered to be the traditional dress of the English countryman. A few of these smocks, beautifully embroidered, are still preserved. His gaiters are derived from the SPATTERDASHES shown on Page 65.

The farm bailiff is dressed in knee-breeches fastened *à pont*, a jacket slightly full in the skirt, and a double-breasted waistcoat. His high collar and CRAVAT are in formal contrast to the knotted NECKERCHIEF of the farm hand. Gaiters could be either knee-length or reaching mid-thigh, as shown.

Over their high-waisted gowns women wore a short jacket called a SPENCER, reputed to have been named after Lord Spencer, who accidentally burned the tails off his coat, thus creating a new fashion. Men sometimes wore short SPENCERS over their tail-coats. An additional garment for warmth was the PELERINE, a small shoulder-cape similar to that worn in medieval times (17).

Farm labourers and other kinds of workmen often wore short, sleeveless waistcoats, and spotted NECKERCHIEFS.

FARM HAND
1815

FARM BAILIFF
1815

LONG
GAITERS
1815

1815

PELERINE

SPENCER

LABOURER
1815

The lady of 1815 on **Page 71** is wearing styles fashionable at the time of the Battle of Waterloo. While her dress is still high waisted, under her PELISSE or coat, skirts were gradually becoming fuller. Her high-crowned bonnet was known as the BIBI BONNET. Shoes still took the form of flat pumps.

The man-about-town wears yellow NANKEEN trousers; it is thought that these loose trousers originated from those worn by poorer French Revolutionaries. His cut-away coat is collared and cuffed in velvet. The top hat had now replaced the BEAVER. Men as well as women wore flat pumps or ESCARPINES. Shirt-collars were stiff and high, worn with dark CRAVATS and frilled shirt-fronts.

At evening parties, routs, and assemblies, ladies usually wore gay turbans trimmed with a small plume or ESPRIT. By 1821 top hats had become very tall in the crown.

As yet another variation of ladies' millinery, beribboned straw hats were adapted from bonnets.

LADY
1815

MAN-ABOUT-TOWN
1818

TURBAN
1815

TOP HAT

1821

HAT
1823

71

By the 1820s the waistline of dresses had descended to its normal position and skirts had become fuller, as worn by the lady of 1825 on **Page 73**. Sleeves were very full at the top, narrowing to the lower arm, a style which became known as the MAMELUKE sleeve, similar to the LEG O' MUTTON or GIGOT sleeve fashionable in the Victorian period(79). Large, much-decorated hats, which remind one of those worn just before the First World War, were popular at this time. Flat pumps were still worn.

Evening dress in 1825 featured tight PANTALOONS, cut-away coats, fancy waistcoats, and frilled shirts. High collars and CRAVATS were still worn. Patent leather was invented during this period and men wore evening pumps similar to those still worn in modern times.

The business man wears a tightly waisted overcoat; in order to achieve or preserve a slim, elegant silhouette, plump gentlemen wore corsets or waistcoats laced tightly at the back. Long trousers were now customary wear, with heeled shoes during the day.

Ladies' hats were tall crowned as coiffures were still dressed high. Except for a brief period when children wore the charming and simple clothes shown in the portraits painted by Gainsborough, Romney, and Raeburn, girls' and boys' clothes were merely miniature copies of those of their elders. The girl of 1832 is wearing long, lace-trimmed PANTALETTES. The boy of 1832 is dressed in a tightly waisted overcoat with MAMELUKE sleeves.

By about 1820, because of the smoke and dirt from the increasing number of factories, men no longer wore clothes in gay colours and materials. Thus began the custom of wearing sober hard-wearing black, brown, grey, and dark blue, colours which still predominate in men's fashions. Having regard to the English climate, a very important discovery took place in 1825—the invention and patenting of waterproof cloth by Mr. Charles Macintosh.

Materials

Up to 1780: Velvet, satin, taffeta, and brocade.
Lutestring (ribbed silk).
Paduasoy (thick corded silk from Padua).
Chintz.
Calico (Indian cotton material from Calicut).
Camlet (fine woollen).
Linsey-woolsey (coarse cotton and wool mixture).
Linen.

1780–1837: Broadcloth (for men's coats).   Muslin.
Gauze.   Levantine and broche silk.
Checked and plaid woollens.
Merino and cashmere.

Predominant colours

Up to 1780: Bright flower and jewel colours, pastels and 'hunting pink'.
After 1780: Darker, rich colours for men's coats—bottle-green, King's blue, claret, russet, mulberry, snuff-colour (grey-brown).
After 1820: Black, grey, brown, dark blue.
For women: white, pale flower colours, celestial blue, amaranth (purple).

EVENING DRESS
1825

BUSINESS
MAN
1825

LADY
1825

HAT
1825

GIRL
1832

BOY
1832

9 The Victorians 1837–1900

During the long reign of Queen Victoria, Great Britain settled down to a period of solid respectability and prosperity, after the rakish era of the Regency. This reaction was symbolized in the costume of the period, in the solid, pyramidal silhouettes of women in their wide CRINOLINES and in the sober, hard-wearing garments worn by men. Between the extremes of wealth and poverty of the upper and the poorest working classes stood that large section of the community, the middle class, consolidated by the Industrial Revolution. Because of the many mechanical inventions in the spinning and weaving trades developed since the end of the 18th century, a far wider range of materials was available to everyone, the governing factor of quality being that of finance rather than rank and social status.

The lady of 1837 shown on **Page 75** illustrates the fashionable 'hour glass' silhouette of the period, her dress being very wide at the shoulders, accentuated by large MAMELUKE sleeves; these and increasingly wide skirts emphasized a slim waist achieved in many cases by rigid corsetry, no doubt the cause of many ladylike swoons and 'having the vapours'.

Skirts increased in width, as worn by the lady of 1840. They were held out by a great number of petticoats; first came one of flannel, then one stiffened with horsehair, followed by cotton stiffened with braid, another with horsehair-stiffened flounces, and yet one or two more of starched muslin. It is probable that the sheer weight of these garments might have caused wide skirts to die out had it not been for the invention of the lighter CRINOLINE frame(77). The lady of 1840 is wearing a PELISSE with hanging sleeves. As further evidence of the fact that there are constant revivals and adaptations of old styles in fashion, see Page 19.

The cook, still wearing a MOB CAP in 18th-century style, is dressed in a full-skirted cotton gown, which may be taken as the typical and long-established garb of domestic workers. Boys of 1840 might wear either caps or large, floppy berets, as illustrated.

The business man wears a loose, short overcoat as a variation from a longer one fitting closely at the waist. His trousers are strapped under the instep.

Tall felt bowler hats or PLUGS were popular in 1855; men wore their hair long and adorned their faces with luxuriant 'mutton-chop' whiskers, 'Dundreary whiskers' or 'Piccadilly weepers'. By the 1860s a small, shallow version of the bowler hat was fashionable.

LADY
1837

LADY
1840

COOK
1845

CAP
1840

BOWLER HAT
1855

BUSINESS MAN
1850

BOWLER HAT
1866

BERET
1840

75

As shown on **Page 77**, by 1860 the CRINOLINE reached its maximum width. Its wearer is dressed in a PELISSE over her gown. The discovery of aniline dyes by a Mr. Perkin in 1856 had a startling effect on the colour of clothes worn by the Victorian matron; in their early stages the dyes were crude and bright, and tended to rot materials. The invention of the sewing-machine at this time made the task of seamstresses and dressmakers easier, and also enabled housewives to make more clothes at home.

The foundation of the CRINOLINE was a graduated series of bamboo, whalebone, or metal hoops held together with strips of stout material. A small, wasp-waisted corset was worn over a chemise and long frilled drawers. Striped stockings were often worn. On her head this model wears a netted SNOOD.

Bonnets varied a great deal in style; the CAPOTE shape was popular at this time. Caps were usually worn indoors by married women; it was customary for them to wear bonnets in lieu of small, frivolous hats as a mark of their status, when walking out.

The young girl of 1862 wears a short CRINOLINE, displaying her lace-trimmed PANTALETTES. The girl of 1865 wears a 'pork-pie' hat and netted SNOOD; note her elastic-sided boots with patent-leather toe-caps. These had been invented in 1836.

The gleaner is wearing a traditional English sun-bonnet. The farm labourer's clothes are typical of those worn by the working classes: spotted NECKERCHIEF, loose waistcoat, and homespun trousers tied at the knees.

Victorian ladies attached great importance to the wearing of gloves, even at night, to keep their hands soft and white.

CRINOLINE
1860

FOUNDATION of CRINOLINE
1860

CAPOTE
1860

CAP

1865

1870

GIRL
1862

GIRL
1865

GLEANER 1868

FARM
LABOURER

77

By 1870 the BUSTLE had replaced the CRINOLINE, as illustrated on **Page 79.** Maybe it evolved by discarding hoops, pushing the surplus material of skirts to the back and draping it over a pad of horsehair or metal springs. In the late 1870s the BUSTLE was not high fashion, being briefly replaced by the straight 'princess line', but it returned to favour in the 1880s. Small feathered hats replaced bonnets. The middle-class housewife of 1879 wears a high-necked dress with tucked bodice, pleated skirt, and draped BUSTLE.

The business man is dressed in what was virtually the uniform of the 'city gentleman', i.e. FROCK-COAT trimmed with braid and silk lapels, striped trousers, stiff collar, CRAVAT, and top hat.

For sporting occasions the checked or plaid INVERNESS CAPE and DEER-STALKER hat were popular, and are associated with a certain Mr. Sherlock Holmes. The boy of 1889 wears a sailor suit and cap, his KNICKERBOCKERS being knee-length, showing woollen stockings.

By 1890 the BUSTLE had disappeared in favour of a simpler, straight skirt as worn by the housewife. Once again, LEG O' MUTTON sleeves were in fashion.

The middle-class man is wearing a SACK SUIT, usually of checked or pepper-and-salt material, which had first become popular in the 1880s as a more loosely fitting and comfortable alternative to formal business clothes. From this developed the modern lounge suit.

The grandmother of 1890 is dressed in what was almost the uniform of elderly ladies, a full-skirted black dress, black cape trimmed with jet beadwork, and a small black bonnet.

The elder girl of 1894 shows that high collars and LEG O' MUTTON sleeves were not reserved for grown-ups.

The younger girl of 1894 wears a silk sash over her serge dress.

The cycling outfit of 1896 was considered very daring, and even down-right immodest, as it involved wearing BLOOMERS, named after an American campaigner for freer clothing for women, one Amelia Bloomer. Women were becoming increasingly independent and emancipated, taking part in sport and jobs outside the home; their clothes reflected this social change. As shown by the illustration of the lady of 1900, jackets and skirts became popular; maybe this fashion was considered yet another infringement of the male prerogative of wearing a suit.

Materials Men: Serge, broadcloth, drill, checked and plaid woollens.
Women: Muslin, lawn, tarlatan, gingham, red flannel, taffeta, watered silk, velvet, tulle, alpaca, bombazine, serge.
Colours As in previous period. After 1856—crude and bright aniline dyes.

BUSTLE 1875

HOUSEWIFE 1879

BUSINESS MAN

INVERNESS CAPE 1885

BOY 1889

1880

HOUSEWIFE

MIDDLE-CLASS MAN 1890

GRANDMOTHER 1890

CYCLING OUTFIT 1896

1890

GIRL 1894

GIRL 1894

LADY 1900

10 National Costumes of the United Kingdom and Eire

Ancient Irish

Records of ancient Irish dress of pre-Norman times, that is, prior to Strongbow's Invasion in 1170, have been found in sculpture, metal-work on shrines, and in illuminated manuscripts, a famous example of which is the Book of Kells dating from the 8th century A.D. It would seem that the two main garments worn by persons of any importance were the LÉINE, a long, closely fitting tunic, and the BRAT, an outer mantle. The chief shown on **Page 81** is wearing these garments. At this time folk went barefoot.

From figures carved on the Cross of Muiredach it appears that men of lesser importance wore an alternative form of dress, i.e. a closely fitting sleeveless INAR or jacket adorned with a large kite-shaped brooch, and a pair of short TRIÚS or trews decorated with vertical bands or stripes. The sculptured figures referred to above are soldiers.

Another form of dress for peasants and labourers, not illustrated here, is simply a loin-cloth reaching to the knees, with no other item of clothing except a piece of cloth draped round the shoulders. The Book of Kells includes illustrations of closely fitting jackets and both long and short trews; long trews were strapped under the instep. It is recorded that Harald Gille, who went from Ireland to Norway in 1127, wore 'a shirt and trousers which were bound with ribands under his foot-soles', with a short cloak. From all the information available it may be concluded that the LÉINE was never worn with jacket and trews; the BRAT and LÉINE were almost invariably worn together; the former could be worn as an extra protective garment over jacket and trews. No head-dress other than a military helmet appears; hair was always worn long and seems to have been sufficient protection.

The chief's daughter wears a BRAT and LÉINE girdled with a CRISS. There is no evidence of undergarments, and the BRAT was useful as a blanket or covering at night.

By the 14th century Irish dress was still primitive compared with that of England at the same date. The peasant of 1300 bears a remarkable resemblance to the Ancient British man (11).

The dancer is based on a drawing kept in the Public Record Office in London. The baggy breeches and fantastic hood trimmed with bells are more likely to have been a fancy dress than everyday clothes. The peasant of 1500 is based on a drawing by Albrecht Dürer. He wears a LÉINE covered by a BRAT with a shaggy lining.

The 'Wild Irishman' on **Page 83** is wearing a long LÉINE girded with a belt, the surplus material being left pouched at the waist. A typical feature was the long, hanging sleeves. This garment was bright saffron yellow and

CHIEF
Pre-1169

JACKET and SHORT TREWS
Pre-1169

Pre-1169

JACKET

LONG TREWS

CHIEF'S
DAUGHTER
1200

PEASANT
1300

DANCER
1400

1500

PEASANT

over it came a short embroidered jacket; its narrow sleeves were left open down to the wrist to allow the tunic sleeves to hang free. The edge of the jacket was fringed with tabs of material, and the garment was fastened with tapes not buttons. The outer garment is the customary BRAT.

The peasant woman is based on a painting by Lucas de Heere kept in the library of Ghent University. Her enveloping BRAT is light red; her long LÉINE is dark green, covered by an additional garment in light grey-blue. Her head-dress is unusual, its brim being a roll of white linen striped with red. Its shape is identical with military helmets of the period, in common use throughout Europe by the rank and file, and known by the name of CHAPEL-DE-FER (old French for *chapeau*).

A noblewoman of 1570 appears in another watercolour by Lucas de Heere, kept in the British Museum. Although her style of dress may be becoming Anglicized, the long, full hanging sleeves of her LÉINE are traditionally Irish, the sleeves of her light blue over-gown being reduced to mere strips of material. She carries a money-bag at the end of her red and white girdle, and round her neck is a small RUFF, showing English Tudor influence. Over a white pleated head-dress she wears a small red and white hat. Also painted by Lucas de Heere is the citizen's wife, maybe a well-to-do middle-class woman of Waterford or Galway. Her dress is rose-pink with a laced bodice and a looped-up overskirt of fur. Her black felt hat is worn over a pleated white head-dress, a characteristic Irish feature.

The citizen's wife of 1575 could, from a description of women's head-dresses, be a woman of Limerick. The description reads: 'they weare rolles of lynnen, each roll containing twenty bandles of fine lynnen clothe [a bandle is half an ell] and made up in the form of a myter'. The gathered neck of her undergarment may have been influenced by Early Tudor shirts(27). She wears clogs similar to Tudor CHOPINES(39).

The girl of 1575 shows typical hanging sleeves and looped-up skirt. On her head she wears a simple FILLET of material. From Derricke's 'Image of Ireland' drawn in Ulster in 1581, comes the Chief. The LÉINE has ceased to be a long tunic and now resembles a DOUBLET, opening down the front and adorned with a pleated WAIST-RUFF. He still retains, however, his shaggy BRAT. His hat is secured by a loose chinstrap.

The horse-boy, also depicted by Derricke, wears a modified LÉINE with characteristic hanging sleeves.

The strange processional dress of 1617 is taken from drawings made of an Irish procession at Stuttgart. The participants wore skin-tight trews and sleeveless vests, mantles, and conical hats of striped, shaggy cloth.

The gentlewoman of 1643, based on an engraving by Hollar, is wearing a traditional Irish mantle with a shaggy collar or lining, and a white linen kerchief on her head. Like the noblewoman and citizen's wife referred to above, she wears a crucifix.

The dress of the gentleman of 1643 shows pronounced English influence, DOUBLET, breeches, hat, and shoes being in the Stuart fashion of the same

"WILD IRISHMAN"
1540

1540

1570

1570

PEASANT WOMAN

NOBLEWOMAN

CITIZEN'S WIFE

1575

PROCESSIONAL DRESS
1617

GENTLEWOMAN

CHIEF
1581

CITIZEN'S WIFE

GIRL
1575

HORSE-BOY
1581

1643

1643
GENTLEMAN

period. He may, however, be readily identified as Irish by his fringed, shaggy mantle.

Valuable evidence regarding Irish costume has been obtained from garments discovered in bogs in a very fair state of preservation and now kept in the National Museum in Dublin. Three of these are shown ʲᵘ. **Page 85.**

The jacket and trews were found in 1824 in Co. Sligo; the jacket is made of brown, rough woollen homespun of diagonal weave, 43 inches long and fastened with cloth buttons. The full skirt is gored not pleated; the sleeves are made of two pieces of cloth joined at an angle across the elbow to form a permanent bend, and fastened on the underside with 12 small buttons. The collar was presumably meant to stand up. The legs of the trews are of chequered homespun material, the upper part being of light brown cloth cut loosely and fully. With this suit was a long, semicircular mantle, These garments are considered to date from the 15th or 16th centuries.

The second suit shown was found in Co. Tipperary in 1945. It is made of brown woollen cloth ingeniously tailored. The sleeves are open from armhole to wrist and cover the back of the hand. The trews are made of lighter cloth than the jacket, cut on the cross, and held up like modern pyjamas with a cord at the waist. To facilitate putting on and to ensure a snug fit, the back seam is opened at the lower leg, being fastened with buttons. Marks show that garters were worn below the knee. The cap is made of brown, heavy woollen cloth and fastened with two buttons under the chin. Such a cap is described by Luke Gernon in 1620 as follows: 'A frise capp close to his head with two lappets to button under his chinne.'

The woman's dress was found in 1843 in Co. Tipperary; it is made of coarse, dark brown woollen homespun. The skirt has 92 gores and measures about 22½ feet round the bottom, the top being finely gathered on to a separate bodice.

Two hats, not illustrated here, were found at Boulebane and are of a yellowish brown thick felt sewn together from separate pieces and covered with shaggy tufts of wool sewn on. They have wide brims.

Materials   Coarse woollens.
                Bleached linen.
   Colours   Bright (*gel*) colours obtained from vegetable dyes, but no evidence of tartans.
                Saffron yellow, purple, crimson, green, blue, black grey, dun, striped, and variegated.

The Isle of Man

No ancient Manx literature is available from which details of ancient costume may be obtained. However, it seems logical to assume that as the island was Gaelic in speech and culture by the 9th century and had strong links with both Ireland and Scotland, ancient Manx costume was similar to that worn by these Gaelic peoples. Details of peasant costumes worn during the last century are known; some are shown on **Page 85.**

CLOTHING DISCOVERED *in* IRISH BOGS

Found 1824

Found 1945

Found 1843

TRADITIONAL COSTUMES *of the* ISLE OF MAN

Men wore either knee-breeches or loose homespun trousers, with long knitted footless stockings (OASHYR VOYNEE or OASHYR-SLOBBAGH) similar to Irish trews. The earlier form of these reached the thigh and had one foot-strap under the heel and another under the toes. The later form reached the knee, with only one strap under the instep. Men wore either form; women usually wore the shorter. Breeches were kept up with a CRISS or girdle, this being a long knitted band of brightly coloured wool 2 or 3 inches wide, long enough to pass twice round the body before tying. Shirts were made of flannel or linen, covered by a loose, short jacket. Either tall beaver hats or knitted caps similar to Scottish bonnets were worn. An additional garment for warmth was a cloak or plaid. Shoes or CARRANES were of rough calf-skin with the hair left on, fastened with leather thongs, and, for extra warmth, an inner sole of sheepskin was attached with pitch. Women often went barefoot, although they also wore OASHYR VOYNEE and CARRANES, especially the older women. Petticoats were of red linsey-woolsey, under wide, heavy flannel skirts pleated into the waistband. Skirts were usually blue or, in the south of the island, dark red (a lichen dye). The bodice or GOON LHIABBEE was a loose jacket of dyed linen with a broad collar. A blue and white checked linen apron, a white KERCHIEF fastened at the neck with a brooch, and a cap or COIF COOIL CORRAN, worn both in and out of doors by older women, completed the ensemble. Additional garments were the older women's triangular knitted shawl, crossed in front and tied at the back, and a long circular hooded cloak of homespun. Sun-bonnets were worn in summer.

There were no tartans but 'Manx plaid', in small checks of scarlet and bright blue, was popular in country districts.

Colours Men: Green, grey, and brown obtained from vegetable dyes.
Women: Blue and red.

Scottish

Information regarding ancient Scottish costume before the 16th century is very scanty; early Christian sculpture throws some light on the subject. Roman writers commented on the skill of early Celtic tribes in weaving good woollen cloth in varied colours and stripes. Home-grown vegetable dyes were used and produced beautiful, quiet, and muted colours which blended with the heather and provided good camouflage. There are many similarities between ancient Irish and Scottish costume, and in their shared Gaelic culture. Tartan or BREACHAN (chequered) had developed in its authentic form by 1471; early tartans were simple checks coloured with dyes from roots, berries, and shrubs, made in districts where weaving was the predominant craft. Therefore, particular patterns came to be associated with particular districts and local families; hence the Clan tartans. An ancient method of describing tartan was 'mottled, chequered, striped, sundrie coloured, marled'; weavers took great pains to preserve exact patterns of tartan prescribed by SETTS, on pattern-sticks or MAIDE DALBH.

HIGHLANDERS

1500   1570   1578

1600   1743   1745

SCOTSWOMAN   BELTED PLAIDS   HIGHLAND DRESS

After the unsuccessful rising in favour of Bonnie Prince Charlie in 1745, the Highlanders were disarmed, and in 1746 an English Act of Parliament was passed proscribing the wearing of tartan and making it a penal offence. The Act was not repealed until 1782, by which time the old weavers were dead, the original SETTS lost, and the traditional pattern-sticks rotted away. However, fragments of original tartans were preserved and new patterns evolved, and by 1822, George IV encouraged a great revival of interest.

The chief feature of ancient Scottish dress worn by the Highlanders, as illustrated on **Page 87**, was the saffron shirt. That of the Highlander of 1500 is quilted with wool and daubed with grease or pitch as waterproofing. He wears a heavy mantle, of shaggy frieze as in Ireland, but often of plaid. His shoes are made of rough, untanned hide, although it was common for folk to go barelegged and barefooted. Alternatively, CUARAN or knee-length boots were worn, made from horse- or cow-hide and kept up with thongs. Hair was allowed to grow thick and long, and no head-dress was worn in early days; gradually a knitted woollen bonnet was adopted, bearing the Clan badge of a flower or plant.

The Highlander of 1570 is based on a drawing by Lucas de Heere. He is wearing a chequered jacket and short trews, enveloped in an unpatterned mantle, and with leather brogues on his feet. His weapons are a large claymore and a dagger.

The Highlander of 1578 is based on a description of dress written by Bishop Lesley, and bears very strong resemblance to ancient Irish costume (83). He wears a linen shirt with wide trailing sleeves, dyed with saffron among the rich, smeared with grease among the poor; over this comes a short woollen jacket with open sleeves. His long trews are chequered.

It is not easy to find details of women's dress; certainly, when considering Highland costume, the honours go to the men. The Scotswoman of 1600 wears a long gown or ARASAID of plaid or tartan belted at the waist. A TONNAG or small square of woollen material is draped over her shoulders and fastened with a brooch. On her head is a CURRAICHD of linen, tied under her chin.

The saffron shirt went out of favour in 1600 and did not reappear. After considerable discussion and conjecture, it is accepted that the belted plaid is the origin of the kilt or PHILABEG. With the disappearance of the saffron shirt or tunic the plaid became necessary to cover and protect the body below the waist. The illustrations of the belted plaid are based on engravings of men of the Black Watch made in 1743 by Van der Gucht. The plaid was a length of tartan cloth about 5 feet wide and 12 to 18 feet in length, pleated to suit the wearer's girth and belted at the waist so that the lower half reached the knees. Having put on his jacket, the wearer draped the upper half over his shoulders in bad weather; otherwise the left corner was fastened to the left shoulder with a brooch, pin, or button, the rest of the upper half of the plaid being draped at the back, and tucked into the belt so that none of it was visible at the front.

JACKET and TREWS
1746

BOY
Pre-1746

BOY
Pre-1746

HIGHLAND DRESS
1850

89

The jacket worn with Highland dress in 1745 is slashed in front and on the sleeves. Stockings are tied with garters. It is recorded that ladies wore plaids, gracefully draped to cover their heads if necessary.

The jacket and trews of 1746 shown on **Page 89** are reputed to have been worn by Prince Charles Edward Stuart, the Young Pretender, at the Battle of Culloden. The pre-proscription period tartan is a gay one, the SETT of the warp running as follows:

White	12 threads	Yellow	8 threads
Blue	2 threads	Green	40 threads
Black	12 threads	Violet	8 threads
Red	16 threads	Black	35 threads
Yellow	8 threads	Violet	8 threads
White	4 threads	Red	30 threads
Black	8 threads	Blue	27 threads
White	4 threads		

(The violet is pale in colour, the dye being obtained from wild cress.)

The collar and cuffs of the jacket are of purple velvet, and the buttons of bone covered with silver embossed with the Stuart rose. The jacket is lined with red woollen material. The trews, cut on the cross, are patterned with red and green checks.

It was common for several tartans to be worn simultaneously, as illustrated in the drawings of boys (based on a portrait of the MacDonald children) of the pre-proscription period.

During Victorian times, tremendous interest was shown in tartans, encouraged by the Queen. The Highland dress of 1850 approximates to the modern full-dress version.

Colours Saffron, soft green, brown, grey, and violet, from vegetable dyes. Bright red, blue, green, yellow, black, and purple from aniline dyes after 1856.

Materials Linen, woollen, drugget (mixed linen and wool—for women's garments).

Welsh

Authentic details of traditional costume are scanty; an early 17th-century manuscript refers in an inventory to linen smocks, aprons, PARTLETS (NECKERCHIEFS or RUFFS), flannel jerkins and petticoats, woollen KERSIE stockings white and dyed, shoes, a silk girdle, linen and strings for RUFFS, fringe for petticoats, a FILLET for the hair, gloves, and a felt hat. As far as Scottish costume is concerned, men steal the limelight, but in Wales interest seems to be focused on women's dress; presumably men's clothing showed no peculiarly Welsh characteristics and differed little from English styles. Rather than an overall form of Welsh national costume, there were variations in different localities, although a basic style of gown with fitting bodice and full skirt appears to have been general.

PEASANT WOMAN
1815

WOMAN of
CARDIGAN

1830

1810

GIRL from
CHARITY SCHOOL

1830

WOMEN of GWENT

1831

The peasant woman shown on **Page 91** wears a gown and skirted jacket of striped woollen material. The Celtic peoples were traditionally fond of striped and of plaid materials from very early times (9). Her shawl is crossed at the front and tied at the back; her cap is utilitarian rather than stylish, and as she is a washerwoman doing her work by a stream her feet are protected by heavy wooden SABOTS. Her stockings are of hand-knitted homespun wool, striped in this instance, but usually white, black, or dark blue. The girl of 1810 from a Welsh Charity school in London is based on a contemporary lithograph. Her apron has a deep circular collar and she carries a voluminous cape. Over her cap she would wear a wide-brimmed hat or bonnet.

The woman of Cardigan is dressed in a double-skirted gown with a blue checked apron. Her hat disproves the theory that Welsh women always wore tall STEEPLE-CROWNED hats similar to those of the Puritans (47). Although this style is featured in modern versions of Welsh national costume, shallower hats, or top hats identical with men's, were popular. It was customary for women to wear frilled white cambric or linen caps beneath their hats. Their usual type of shoe was a flat pump of plain black leather.

Local fashions in millinery, as worn in the 1830s in Gwent, show that variations took place within a locality.

Page 93 illustrates the costume of a woman of Gower. Under a full-skirted jacket of checked material she wears a wide skirt. In this district, too, the frilled cap with long LAPPETS is worn under a top hat. The fisherman carrying his coracle is wearing a striped smock and long trousers, with a sou'wester-type hat. The barefoot girl of 1836 wears a high-waisted dress, showing her long-sleeved CHEMISE.

The countrywoman of 1850 is based on a contemporary lithograph. Her caped, fur-trimmed cloak affords ample protection, worn over her full-skirted gown and apron. Her frilled cap frames her face, and the crown of her tall hat is slightly tapering. The next countrywoman of 1850 shows the small triangular shawl commonly worn, made of fine woollen material patterned with spots, checks, or in the traditional Paisley design.

The elderly woman of 1851 wears white and patterned KERCHIEFS under her shallow, wide-brimmed hat. The countrywoman of 1852 wears a striped shawl.

By 1830 the wearing of traditional Welsh costume was beginning to decline in favour of pretty, flimsy materials, gay straw bonnets, fashionable frills and furbelows; this was loudly lamented by a Lady Llanover in 1834.

Colours Black, white, dark blue, red, and yellow.
Materials Homespun woollen cloth.
Flannel.
Linen.
Cambric.

WOMAN of GOWER 1830

FISHERMAN 1850

1850

GIRL 1836

COUNTRYWOMAN

1850

1851

1852

COUNTRYWOMEN'S HATS

Bibliography

The Story of Clothes by Agnes Allen (Faber & Faber).

Gallery of English Costume (Art Galleries Committee, Manchester).

Discovering Costume by Audrey I. Barfoot (University of London Press Ltd.).

Historic Costume for the Stage by Lucy Barton (A. & C. Black).

World Costumes by Angela Bradshaw (A. & C. Black).

History of English Costume by Iris Brooke (A. & C. Black).

A Pictorial History of Costume by Wolfgang Bruhn and Max Tilke (Zwemmer).

English Costume, 1066–1820 by Dion Clayton Calthrop (A. & C. Black).

The Perfect Lady by C. Willet Cunningham (Max Parrish).

Costume Cavalcade by Henny Harald Hansen (Methuen).

Costume of the Western World Series (Harrap).

Ancient Greek, Roman and Byzantine Costume and Decoration by Mary G. Houston (A. & C. Black).

Medieval Costume in England and France by Mary G. Houston (A. & C. Black).

A Short History of Costume and Armour, 1066–1800 by Kelly and Schwabe (Batsford).

The Changing Shape of Things Series—Dress by James Laver (Murray).

Old Irish and Highland Dress by H. F. McClintock (Dundalgan Press (W. Tempest) Ltd.).

Welsh Costume and Customs (The National Library of Wales).

A History of Everyday Things in England by Marjorie and C. H. B. Quennell (Batsford).

English Fashion by Alison Settle (Collins).

Historic Costuming by Nevil Truman (Pitman).

English Costume from the Second Century B.C. to 1950 by Doreen Yarwood (Batsford).

Outline of English Costume by Doreen Yarwood (Batsford).

Index

The numbers in **bold** type denote the page numbers of illustrations